Cookbook Recipes for cancer patients

Nutritious Recipes for healing and treating cancer

Irene .B. white

TABLE OF CONTENT

Chapter 1

Eating Right to fight Cancer

Did you know that you can lower your risk of developing cancer? According to the International Agency for Research on Cancer, there will be 29.5 million additional cancer cases diagnosed annually in the United States by 2040. Numerous of these incidents, according to research, could be avoided.

Even while research into cancer prevention is ongoing, we do know that your lifestyle decisions can have an impact on your risk of acquiring cancer. In fact, according to recent studies, food and exercise may be responsible for up to one-third of all cancer deaths. Aside from giving up smoking and shielding your skin from UV radiation, some of the most significant things you can do to lower your chance of developing cancer include eating healthily and engaging in regular physical activity throughout your life.

Here are some general guidelines for lowering your cancer risk through proper nutrition.

Consume a lot of fruits and vegetables, which have been linked to a lower risk of certain cancers. Fill half of your plate with colorful fruits and vegetables at each meal.

Reduce your consumption of highly processed,low-nutritional foods. Consuming foods high in added sugars and saturated fats leaves little room for foods high in nutrients.

Cancer-fighting foods You can still eat the foods you enjoy, but they should be whole grains, vegetables, fruit, nuts, seeds, and lean protein foods.

Concentrate on plant proteins. Beans and lentils are high-protein, low-cost sources of fiber and fiber. Consuming a lot of red, processed, and charred meat has been linked to an increased risk of cancer, so eat it sparingly.

Consume alcohol in moderation. All types of alcoholic beverages may increase your risk of breast, colorectal, and other types of cancer, according to research. If you are of legal drinking age and choose to consume alcohol, limit your intake to one drink or less per day for women and two drinks or less per day for men on days when alcohol is consumed.

Chapter 2

What better way to start the day than with an energizing breakfast full of healthy, delicious ingredients?

1.Turmeric Tofu Scrambled with Greens

Ingredients
- 114-ounce package extra firm tofu
- 2 tablespoons nutritional yeast
- 2 teaspoons turmeric
- ½ teaspoon smoked paprika
- ¼ teaspoon black pepper
- Pinch sea salt (optional)
- 2 tablespoons plain, unsweetened soymilk
- 1 tablespoon extra virgin olive oil
- 2 green onions, sliced
- 2 cloves garlic, minced

- 6 ounces (about 2–1/4 cups) sliced mushrooms
- 2 cups loosely packed chopped greens (i.e., mustard, collard, spinach, kale)
- ¼ cup sun-dried tomatoes, chopped

Methods

- Remove tofu from package, and press it by wrapping it in paper towels and placing it between two plates with something heavy on top for 5 minutes, to allow extra liquid to drain off tofu.

- Place tofu in a bowl and crumble with your hands to achieve a crumbly texture. Mix in nutritional yeast, turmeric, smoked paprika, black pepper, salt (optional), and soymilk.

- Heat olive oil in a skillet and sauté green onions, garlic, and mushrooms for about 5 minutes.

- Add crumbled tofu, chopped greens, and sun-dried tomatoes and sauté just until greens start to wilt (about 2 minutes). Serve immediately. May serve with sliced avocados, if desired.

- Makes 6 servings (about ¾ cup each)

2.Chickpea Pancakes with Almond Butter and Jelly Berry Grape Jam.

Ingredient

For the Jam:
- 2 cups purple grapes, cut in half
- 2 Tbsp. lemon juice
- 1 tsp. honey
- 1/4 tsp. ground cinnamon
- Pinch of salt. or to taste
- 1 tsp. cornstarch
- 1 Tbsp. water

For the Pancakes:
- 1 cup chickpea flour
- 2 tsp. baking powder
- 1/4 tsp. ground cinnamon
- Pinch of salt, or to taste
- 3/4 cup plain unsweetened almond milk
- 1 tsp. honey
- 1/2 tsp. vanilla extract
- Nonstick cooking spray
- 4 Tbsp. almond or peanut butter

Directions
- Place a small saucepan over medium heat. Add grapes, lemon juice, honey, cinnamon and salt and stir to combine. Bring to low boil, lower heat, and simmer, uncovered, stirring occasionally, until grapes soften, about 8 minutes.

- Place cornstarch and water in a small bowl and whisk to combine. Stir into grape mixture and cook, stirring frequently, until thickened, 1 to 2 minutes. Set aside.

- Meanwhile, place chickpea flour, baking powder, cinnamon and salt in a medium-size bowl and whisk until well combined. Whisk in almond milk, honey and vanilla until well combined.

- Spray a 10-inch nonstick skillet with nonstick cooking spray and heat over medium heat. Pour in 1/3 cup of batter and cook until golden on the bottom, 2 to 3 minutes. Adjust heat to medium-low if bottom browns too quickly. Flip and cook for another 2 minutes. Repeat with cooking spray and remaining batter. Keep pancakes warm between batches.

- To serve, spread 1 tablespoon almond butter evenly over each pancake. Top evenly with Jellyberry grape jam.

3. **Fresh Fruit and Oatmeal**

INGREDIENTS
- ¾ cup rolled oats
- ¼ teaspoon ground cinnamon
- Pinch of sea salt
- ¼ cup fresh berries (optional)
- ½ ripe banana, sliced (optional)
- 2 tablespoons chopped nuts, such as walnuts, pecans, or cashews (optional)
- 2 tablespoons dried fruit, such as raisins, cranberries, chopped apples, chopped
- Apricots (optional)
- Maple syrup (optional)

INSTRUCTIONS
- Combine the oats and 1½ cups water in a small saucepan. Bring to a boil

over high heat. Reduce the heat to medium-low and cook until the water has been absorbed, about 5 minutes.
- Stir in the cinnamon and salt. Top with the berries, banana, nuts, and/or dried fruit, as you like. If desired, pour a little maple syrup on top. Serve hot.

4. Herbed Chickpea Crepes with Spinach and Mushroom

Ingredients

Crepes:
- 1 cup chickpea flour
- 2 Tbsp. extra-virgin olive oil
- 1 tsp. finely chopped fresh rosemary
- 1/4 tsp. salt
- 1 cup water
- 2 tsp. soft buttery spread, if using skillet

Filling:
- 2 tsp. extra-virgin olive oil
- 1/4 cup finely chopped red onion

- 1/3 cup finely chopped red bell pepper
- 6 oz. cremini mushrooms, thinly sliced (about 2 cups)
- 1 box (5oz.) baby spinach
- 2 Tbsp. prepared pesto
- Salt and freshly ground black pepper, to taste

Directions

- In a medium bowl, whisk chickpea flour, oil, rosemary and salt with 1 cup water until mixture is smooth. Let the batter sit for 20-30 minutes to thicken. Before cooking, stir to loosen any clumps.
- For crepes, set a non-stick pan over medium-high heat until drops of water flicked into the pan ball up and bounce. With one hand, hold the pan up at a 45-degree angle. Pour ¼ cup batter near top of pan, rotating pan as you pour so batter flows into 6-7-inch round crepe. Cook until the crepe is golden on bottom, 1-2 minutes. Using

a large spatula, flip and cook until the crepe is lightly golden on bottom, about 30 seconds. Transfer crepe to a large plate. Cover each crepe with wax paper.

- If not filling crepes immediately, cool to room temperature and cover the plate with plastic wrap. Hold crepes at room temperature for up to 8 hours, refrigerate for up to 24 hours.

- For filling, in a medium skillet heat oil over medium-high heat. Add onion and cook, stirring for 2 minutes. Add red peppers and cook, stirring, until onions are translucent, 5 minutes. Add mushrooms and cook, stirring occasionally, until mixture looks wet, 5-6 minutes. Add spinach, stirring to wilt leaves. Cook, stirring often, until most of the moisture has evaporated and the filling is tender, 8 minutes.

- If crepes have been made ahead, wrap them in foil and warm at 250 degree F for 20 minutes. To assemble crepes, in a small bowl, mix pesto with 2 tbsp. warm water. Stir pesto into the filling. Arrange a crepe on a plate. Spoon ⅙ filling over bottom half of each crepe, then gently fold crepe in half over filling. Repeat with remaining crepes and filling. If desired, garnish the plate with some mesclun leaves and strawberries. Serve immediately.

5. Cottage Cheese, Cucumber, and Tomato Toast

Ingredients
- 1 slice whole grain bread
- ¼ cup reduced fat cottage cheese
- 4-5 thin cucumber slices
- 2-3 thin tomato slices, cut into quarters

- Cracked black pepper (to taste)

Directions

- Toast bread.
- Spread cottage cheese on bread.
- Top with cucumber slices, tomato slices, and

6. Peanut Butter Toast with Banana and Chia Seeds

Ingredients

- 1 slice whole grain bread
- 1 Tbsp. peanut butter
- 1/2 banana, sliced
- 1 tsp. chia seed (or flaxseed)
- 1 g added sugar.

Directions

- Toast bread.
- Spread peanut butter on toast.
- Top with sliced banana and chia seed

Snacks high in protein

What is the significance of protein?

Protein is essential for fighting infections and improving immunity.
It helps to keep your body fluids balanced and transports your medication to all parts of your body.
It also aids in the health of your muscles, connective tissues, red blood cells, enzymes, and hormones.

Which foods have the most protein?

There are numerous plant-based protein sources to include in your daily diet:

- Peanuts, almonds, and walnuts are examples of nuts.
- Pumpkin seeds, sunflower seeds, and sesame seeds are examples of seeds

- Lentils (dals), peas, dried beans, and other legumes

Animal-based foods that can help you get enough protein in your diet include:

- Milk, cheese, and curd are examples of dairy products.

- Fish and crabs are examples of sea foods.

- Chicken, quail, and duck are examples of poultry.

Here are three recipes for tasty, high-protein meals to add to your menu;

CHANA DAL DOSA

Cancer protein diet

Chana dal, also known as split Bengal gram or chickpeas, is a popular legume in India. These dosas are a good source of protein for breakfast.

Aside from proteins, this dish is high in vitamin B and phosphorus. It is also suitable for those who are diabetic.

It goes well with green chutney.

Ingredients

- Chana dal (split bengal gram): ½ cup, soaked

- Fenugreek (methi) leaves: ¼ cup, finely chopped

- Carrots: ¼ cup, finely chopped

- Curd: 2 tablespoon

- Ginger & green chili: 1 teaspoon, finely chopped

- Oil: 1 tsp

- Salt as per taste

Method
- Soak the chana for at least a couple of hours, or overnight if possible.
- Grind the soaked chana into a coarse paste, using ¼ cup of water.
- Mix all the remaining ingredients (except oil), including the salt to the batter.
- Heat and oil the tawa (pan), and spread the batter on it.
- Cook till both sides become golden brown by flipping the dosa.

- Serve hot.

Here's another protein-packed vegetarian recipe for breakfast or snacks.

Oats are high in antioxidants and contain the soluble fiber beta-glucan. It is a filling breakfast that is also suitable for those with diabetes and dyslipidemia.

Moong dal, or split green gram, is an excellent source of iron and potassium.

Ingredients
- Split moong dal: ½ cup

- Rolled oats: ½ cup

- Fresh curd:2 tablespoon

- Grated carrot & onion: 2 tablespoon

- Ginger garlic paste: 1 tablespoon

- Chili powder: ½ tsp

- Garam masala: ¼ tsp

- Turmeric powder: ¼ tsp

- Coriander leaves chopped: 1 tablespoon
- Oil: 2 teaspoon
- Salt to taste

Method
- Boil the split moong dal in water till soft.
- Drain the soft moong dal.
- Grind it into a coarse dough.
- Now add all ingredients (except oil) to the dough.

- Mix the dough well and divide it into flat, round portions.
- Grease the tawa (pan) with oil and cook the tikkis on it.
- Flip them, till they are golden brown on both sides.
- You can serve these with mint or tomato chutney.

Chickpea Pancakes

Chickpea flour or besan are high in proteins. It is also a good source of fibre, minerals and vitamins.

These pancakes are easy to make and you can add vegetables and herbs of your choice as well to the batter.

Ingredients

- Chickpea flour: 1 cup

- Water: 1 ½ cup

- Carrot: 1, finely grated

- Spring onion: 1, finely chopped (alternatively you can use an onion)

- Turmeric: ¼ tsp

- Cumin seeds: ¼ tsp

- Salt: ¼ tsp

- Coriander: 1 tbsp finely chopped

- Oil: 1 – 2 tbsp

Method

- In a mixing bowl, take the chickpea four and add water while mixing well to avoid lumps.
- In a frying pan, add 1 tbsp of oil.
- Stir fry the carrots, spring onion and the coriander till they are soft. This might take 4 – 5 min.

- Add the fried vegetables and herb to the chickpea batter and mix thoroughly.
- Add the salt to the batter and mix well.
- Heat a pan over medium heat. Drizzle oil.
- Pour a large spoonful of the batter onto the pan and spread evenly, in the shape of a pancake.
- Once pinholes start appearing in the batter, flip the pancake over.
- Once both sides have been cooked, serve with curd, green chutney or a cucumber dip.

Oats Idli

Oatmeal is one of the most nutritionally dense breakfast foods. It is high in proteins as well as fiber and carbohydrates.

Oats idli does not require overnight batter preparation and can be made the day it is served.

Ingredients

- Rolled oats, or instant oats: 1 cup

- Suji rava (fine rava or cream of wheat): ½ cup

- Sour curds: ½ cup

- Water: 1 cup (or as required)

- Coriander : 3 tsp, chopped

For the tempering (or the tadka)

- Oil: ½ tbs

- Mustard seeds: ½ tbs

- Cumin seeds: ½ tbs

- Chana dal: ½ tsp

- Black pepper: ½ tsp, crushed

- Asafoetida or hing: 1 tsp

- Ginger: ½ inch, chopped

- Curry leaves: 1 tsp, chopped

Method

- Powder in the oats in a grinder.
- In a pan, dry roast the suji flour.
- Add the oats flour and stir well over a medium flame, till you can smell the suji flour. Turn off the heat.
- Add the ginger, curry leaves and coriander to it.
- Add the curd and water and mix into a batter of medium consistency.
- Grease idli pans with oil.
- Immediately ladle the batter into the panda and steam in a pressure cooker (without a weight) for 10 – 12 mins.
- Insert a toothpick into the idlis to check if they are cooked thoroughly.
- Serve with coconut chutney or sambar.

Chapter 3

Salad Recipes With Cancer-Fighting Ingredients

Are you interested in learning how to make delicious salads with anti-cancer ingredients? This section of our Guide to Cancer Prevention contains recipes that use anti-cancer ingredients like carrots, raw broccoli, arugula, onions, and tomatoes. Enjoy!

Carrots and avocado salad

Carrots are well-known for their eye-health benefits, but did you know they are also an excellent anti-cancer vegetable? Carrots contain falcarinol, a compound that has been shown to inhibit cancer growth. Researchers discovered that rats with pre-cancerous tumors who were fed carrots were one-third less likely to develop full-scale tumors than the control group..
Avocados in this anti-cancer salad also contain cancer-fighting nutrients like vitamin E and glutathione.

Ingredients

- 1 large peeled, pitted, and diced avocado
- 4 medium peeled and grated carrots
- A squirt of balsamic vinegar
- To taste, sunflower seeds

- To taste, season with salt and freshly ground pepper.

Directions

- Combine avocado and grated carrots in a medium salad bowl. Sprinkle with sunflower seeds, salt, pepper, and balsamic vinegar.
- Cover and refrigerate for at least 20 minutes before serving.

Arugula, Avocado and Tomato Salad

While low in calories, arugula is high in phytochemicals that protect your health. It contains glucosinolates, which are converted into isothiocyanates by the enzyme myrosinase when the plant is chewed.

Isothiocyanates are well known for their ability to neutralize carcinogens and inhibit cancer cell proliferation.

In addition, the tomatoes and avocados in this salad have anti-cancer and antioxidant properties, and the vinegar used to add depth and flavor to the dish contains compounds that can significantly lower the meal's glycemic index rating index.

Low glycemic foods aid in the regulation of insulin and insulin-like growth factor production, both of which can stimulate tumor proliferation, progression, and spread within the body.

Ingredients
- 3 cups young arugula leaves, rinsed
- 2 cups cherry tomatoes, halved
- 1/4 cup sun-dried tomatoes, chopped
- 2 tablespoons extra virgin olive oil
- 1 tablespoon balsamic vinegar

- 2 small avocados, peeled, pitted and sliced

Directions
- In a large plastic bowl with a lid, combine arugula, cherry tomatoes, sun-dried tomatoes, olive oil, and vinegar. Toss well

- Divide onto plates, and top each serving with slices of avocado.

Salad with salmon

This salmon salad is an excellent anticancer meal. Salmon is an excellent source of omega-3 fatty acids and the carotenoid astaxanthin, both of which are thought to protect against cancer. Because of their high concentration of lycopene, a carotenoid with significant antioxidant activity, the cherry tomatoes in this salad also have anti-cancer properties. Furthermore, red onions and capers contain quercetin, a bioflavonoid with anti-cancer, anti-fungal, anti-bacterial, and anti-inflammatory properties.

Ingredients
- 2 large filets wild salmon, either poached or grilled and chilled in the fridge until cool
- 1 cup cherry tomatoes, halved
- 2 red onions, sliced
- 1 tbsp capers
- 1 tablespoon fresh dill, finely chopped
- 1 tbsp balsamic vinegar
- 1 tbsp olive oil

- 1/4 tsp pepper, freshly ground
- Pinch of salt

Directions

- When salmon is cool, remove skin and bones. Break into chunks and add to a bowl.
- Add tomatoes, red onion, and capers. Toss.
- Mix vinegar, olive oil, and dill in a small bowl and add pour over salmon chunks. Toss again.

- Add salt and pepper to taste. Refrigerate for at least 30 minutes before serving.

Chapter 4

What can you drink to avoid getting cancer? The following beverages should be included in a cancer-fighting diet:

1. Coffee In addition to being nutritionally dense, coffee is a concentrated source of antioxidant phytochemicals. Theophylline and theobromine, chlorogenic acid (a powerful phenol), quinic acid, cafestol, and kahweol are among them.

Coffee consumption has been linked to a lower risk of liver, colorectal, endometrial, oral/pharyngeal, and other cancers in some studies.

2. Green, Black, and White Teas Black, green, white, and oolong teas (also known as "true teas") are high in disease-fighting nutrients like catechins and polyphenol

compounds, epigallocatechin gallate (or EGCG), flavonols and more. Researchers believe this is why long-term tea consumption has been linked to lower risks of bladder, stomach, and pancreatic cancers, among others.

Green tea contains a high concentration of EGCG, while other teas contain epicatechin, epigallocatechin (EGC), and epicatechin-3-gallate (ECG). According to an article published in Cancer Metastasis Reviews, "epidemiological studies have reported that green tea consumption may decrease cancer risk."

3. 100 Percent Vegetable Juices
A daily serving of green vegetable juice, or another veggie juice/smoothie with pulp and fiber, is a simple way to increase your nutrient intake and help prevent chronic diseases.

Tomato juice is another beneficial juice because it contains beta carotene/vitamin A, vitamin C, lycopene, and other carotenoids with anti-cancer properties. Lycopene in tomato juice has been linked to prostate cancer prevention.

Carrot juice is high in vitamin C, vitamin K, beta-carotene and alpha-carotene, luteolin, and flavonoid phytochemicals with antioxidant and anti-inflammatory properties.

4. 100 Percent Fruit Juices (No Sugar-Added, In Small Quantities)

According to research, grapefruit juice contains many phytochemicals that help defend against cancer, such as naringenin and other flavonoids, limonin, beta-carotene, lycopene, and vitamin C.

Pomegranate juice contains polyphenols, which have been shown to have antiproliferative, pro-apoptotic, and anti-inflammatory properties, providing protection against prostate, lung, and breast cancers.

According to research, it is critical for fruit juices to be 100 percent fruit with no added sugar and no high fructose corn syrup, because high sugar consumption has been linked to an increased risk of cancer and many other health problems.

5. Herbal Teas
Herbal teas, which include ginger, chamomile, honeybush, dandelion, peppermint, chai, and a variety of Traditional Chinese medicine herbal blends, are caffeine-free and packed with health benefits, including gut health support and inflammation reduction.

"Herbal teas/beverages are high in natural bioactive compounds like carotenoids, phenolic acids, flavonoids, coumarins, alkaloids, and terpenoids." These bioactive compounds possess biological properties such as antioxidant, antibacterial, antiviral, and anti-inflammatory properties.

These teas are also made with water, which has numerous health benefits. Water is beneficial to overall health because it promotes urination and the detoxification of potentially carcinogenic compounds that can accumulate in the bladder and elsewhere..

6. Red Wine (In Moderation)
Resveratrol, which is found in red grapes and red wine, is a cancer-fighting compound. According to research, chemicals found in wine can help to destroy cancer cells and inhibit cancer cell growth.

If You Have Cancer Already

What should cancer patients drink? Doctors recommend the following health-boosting beverages, which can aid in hydration and provide essential nutrients:

- Water. Some cancer treatments may make plain water taste unpleasant; in this case, drink more flavored water, such as mineral water, seltzer water, or water with lemon or other fruit.

- 100% fruit or vegetable juices, which are high in electrolytes and antioxidants and can help prevent dehydration.

- Coconut water or milk, a hydrating beverage high in medium-chain triglycerides, a type of beneficial fatty acid that promotes gut health. Coconut milk (higher in fat) has antibacterial and antioxidant properties that help the immune system.

- Herbal teas, such as ginger tea or peppermint tea, can help with nausea and other treatment-related symptoms.

- Kefir and organic milk (if tolerated) provide numerous vitamins and minerals, as well as probiotics if fermented.

- Bone broth is a one-of-a-kind source of hard-to-find amino acids, collagen, trace minerals, and electrolytes.

If you don't have an appetite, try drinking most liquids at least a half-hour before or after meals to avoid feeling too full.

Keep in mind that caffeine, sugary drinks, and even some fruit juices can cause indigestion, so limit these if diarrhea or nausea occur.